Animal Friends
Two by Two™

Designs by Michele Wilcox

HOUSE of
WHITE
BIRCHES

PUBLISHERS
SINCE 1947

Animal Friends Two by Two

A cherished children's Bible story comes to life in this precious, picture-perfect blanket that is sure to become a family heirloom to treasure for generations. This cheerful Noah's Ark Afghan and the seven huggable stuffed toys that match will delight any baby.

Gerry the Giraffe, Freddie the Fish, Bobby the Bluebird, Leo the Lion, Ellie the Elephant, Terry the Turtle and Madeleine the Monkey are just the right size for a baby to hold. These stuffed toy animals have friendly, smiley faces that welcome any baby to hug them. The unique, very-easy-to-stitch technique for creating legs allows these projects to be worked up quickly.

You'll want to stitch two animals of each kind, so you can enjoy telling your toddler the traditional story of Noah and the ark. In another year, he or she will be telling the story to you, using the animals and the afghan.

This colorful Noah's Ark Afghan with matching stuffed toy animals is sure to please any toddler and his or her mother.

Happy knitting!

Jeanne Stauffer

Jeanne Stauffer, editor

*Madeleine the Monkey, **page 24***
*Ellie the Elephant, **page 26***

Table of Contents

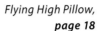

Noah's Ark Afghan, **page 4**

Flying High Pillow, **page 18**

Gerry the Giraffe, **page 11**

Meet the Designer

Michele Wilcox learned to knit when she was 6 years old. Her grandmother, who was a great knitter, crocheter and seamstress, taught her. At first, all she could do was knit every row, so she made a lot of scarves full of holes! As she grew older, she made clothes for her dolls.

She and her friend Ginger taught themselves to crochet when they were 22 years old. She crocheted hundreds of toys for her children when they were small. She would put the toys on their beds at night, and in the morning, they were so surprised! Michele still has some of these toys, and now, her grand-children play with them.

Michele started designing when she wanted to make a certain stuffed toy and couldn't find a pattern for it, so she made her own pattern. That's all it took to discover she loved designing her own projects. She designed a small rabbit and sent the pattern to Annie's Attic. She almost fainted when they bought it. Since that time, she has never stopped designing in both knit and crochet.

Michele said, "I had a great time designing the knitted Noah's Ark blanket and toys."

House of White Birches, Berne, Indiana 46711 DRGnetwork.com

Noah's Ark Afghan

Designs by Michele Wilcox

Skill Level

■■□□ EASY

Finished Size

Approx 34 inches long x 30 inches wide

Materials

- Plymouth Encore Worsted 75% acrylic/25% wool worsted weight yarn (200 yds/100g per ball): 2 balls each yellow #215 (A), teal #9401 (B) and sage green #451 (C); 1 ball each dusty purple #452 (D), denim blue #515 (E), fuchsia #137 (F), orange #1316 (G), pink heather #241 (H) and tan #1203 (I)
- Size 5 (3.75mm) straight and 2 double-pointed needles or size needed to obtain gauge
- Size 9 (5.25mm) circular needle
- Dark brown size 10 crochet thread or pearl cotton
- Tapestry needle
- Fiberfill

Gauge

1 rep pat st = 4 inches/10cm across and 4 ridges on RS of work = 2½ inches on larger needles.

20 sts = 4 inches/10cm in St st on smaller needles. To save time, take time to check gauge.

Special Abbreviation

Increase (inc): Inc 1 st by knitting in front and back of next st.

Pattern Notes

A circular needle is used to accommodate stitches for the afghan. Do not join; work back and forth in rows.

Instructions for working satin stitch, straight stitch and turkey stitch loop embroidery stitches for animals shown on page 31.

Afghan

With larger needle and B, cast on 146 sts.

Row 1 (RS): Knit across.

Row 2: Purl across.

Row 3: K1, *[k2tog] 3 times, [yo, k1] 6 times, [k2tog] 3 times; rep from * to last st, k1.

Row 4: Knit across.

Rows 5–68: Rep [Rows 1–4] 16 times. Cut B, join A.

Rows 69–184: Rep [Rows 1–4] 29 times. Bind off.

Giraffe

With smaller needles and F, cast on 8 sts.

Row 1 (RS): Knit.

Row 2: Purl.

Row 3: Inc, knit to last st, inc—10 sts.

Row 4: Purl.

Rows 5–8: Rep [Rows 3 and 4] twice—14 sts.

Row 9: Knit.

Row 10: Purl.

Row 11: Cast on 3 sts, knit across—17 sts.

Row 12: Purl.

Row 13: Inc, knit across—18 sts.

Row 14: Purl.

Row 15: Knit.

Row 16: Purl.

Row 17: K2tog, knit across—17 sts.

Row 18: Purl.

Row 19: Bind off 3 sts, knit across—14 sts.

Row 20: Purl to last 2 sts, p2tog—13 sts.

Row 21: K2tog, knit across—12 sts.

Rows 22–28: Beg with purl row, work in St st.

Row 29: K1, inc, k10—13 sts.

Row 30: Purl.

Row 31: K11, inc, k1—14 sts.

Row 32: Purl.

Row 33: K1, inc, k12—15 sts.

Row 34: Purl.

Row 35: K13, inc, k1—16 sts.

Row 36: Purl.

Row 37: K1, inc, k14—17 sts.

Row 38: Purl.

Row 39: K15, inc, k1—18 sts.

Rows 40–44: Beg with purl row, work in St st.

Row 45: Knit to last 2 sts, inc, k1—19 sts.

Row 46: Purl.

Row 47: Rep Row 45—20 sts.

Row 48: Purl.

Row 49: Rep Row 45—21 sts.

Row 50: Purl.

Row 51: Rep Row 45—22 sts.

Bind off.

Spots
Make 3

With smaller needles and C, cast on 3 sts.

Row 1: Knit, inc in each st across—6 sts.

Row 2: Knit.

Row 3: [K2tog] 3 times—3 sts.

Bind off.

Sew spots to RS of giraffe.

Ear
With smaller needles and F, cast on 6 sts.

Row 1: Knit.

Row 2: Purl.

Row 3: Knit, inc in each st across—12 sts.

Rows 4–8: Beg with a purl row, work in St st.

Row 9: [K2tog] across—6 sts.

Row 10: Purl.

Row 11: [K2tog] across—3 sts.

Row 12: Purl.

Cut yarn, leaving a long end, thread end through sts and pull tightly. Sew back seam. Do not stuff. Fold Row 1 in half and sew ear in place.

Horn
With smaller needles and C, cast on 5 sts.

Row 1: Knit.

Row 2: Purl.

Cut yarn, leaving a long end, thread end through sts and pull tightly. Sew seam and sew in place.

Face
With dark brown, embroider satin st eye and straight st smile.

Mane
Once giraffe is sewn to afghan, with E, embroider turkey st loops along neck.

Fish
With smaller needles and G, cast on 3 sts.

Row 1 (RS): Knit.

Row 2: Purl.

Row 3: Knit, inc in each st across—6 sts.

Row 4: Purl.

Row 5: Inc, knit to last st, inc—8 sts.

Row 6: Purl.

Row 7: Rep Row 5—10 sts.

Rows 8 and 9: Knit.

Row 10: Purl.

Row 11: Rep Row 5—12 sts.

Rows 12 and 13: Knit.

Row 14: Purl.

Row 15: Rep Row 5—14 sts.

Rows 16 and 17: Knit.

Row 18: Purl.

Row 19: Rep Row 5—16 sts.

Rows 20 and 21: Knit.

Row 22: Purl.

Rows 23–25: Knit.

Row 26: Purl.

Rows 27–29: Knit.

Row 30: Purl.

Row 31: *K2, k2tog; rep from * across—12 sts.

Row 32: Knit.

Row 33: *K1, k2tog; rep from * across—8 sts.

Row 34: Purl.

Row 35: [K2tog] across—4 sts.

Row 36: Knit.

Rows 37–40: Beg with knit row, work in St st.

Row 41: Knit, inc in each st across—8 sts.

Row 42: Purl.

Row 43: Rep Row 41—16 sts.

Row 44: Purl.

Row 45: Inc, knit to last st, inc—18 sts.

Rows 46–50: Beg with purl row, work in St st.

Bind off.

With dark brown, embroider satin st eye and straight st smile.

Top Fin

With smaller needles and G, cast on 10 sts.

Row 1: [K2, p2] twice, k2.

Row 2: [P2, k2] twice, p2.

Rows 3–8: Rep [Rows 1 and 2] 3 times.

Bind off in ribbing. Fold in half and sew in place.

Side Fin

With smaller needles and G, cast on 3 sts.

Row 1: Knit, inc in each st across—6 sts.

Row 2: Purl.

Row 3: Knit.

Row 4: Purl.

Row 5: [K2tog] across—3 sts.

Cut yarn, leaving long end, draw end through rem sts and pull tightly tog. Sew fin on side.

Bird

Beg at head, with smaller needles and E, cast on 4 sts.

Row 1 (RS): Inc, knit to last st, inc—6 sts.

Row 2: Purl.

Rows 3–6: Rep [Rows 1 and 2] twice—10 sts.

Rows 7–10: Beg with knit row, work in St st.

Row 11: [K2tog] across—5 sts.

Row 12: Purl.

Row 13: Knit, inc in each st across—10 sts.

Row 14: Purl.

Row 15: Rep Row 1—12 sts.

Row 16: Purl.

Row 17: Rep Row 1—14 sts.

Rows 18–32: Beg with purl row, work in St st.

Row 33: K2tog, knit to last 2 sts, k2tog—12 sts.

Row 34: Purl.

Row 35: Rep Row 33—10 sts.

Row 36: Purl.

Row 37: Rep Row 33—8 sts.

Rows 38–44: Beg with purl row, work in St st.

Row 45: Rep Row 1—10 sts.

Row 46: Purl.

Row 47: Rep Row 1—12 sts.

Row 48: Purl.

Row 49: Rep Row 1—14 sts.

Row 50: Purl.

Bind off.

With dark brown, embroider satin st eyes.

Run a piece of E yarn 3 rows down from center of tail around center of tail and through again, pull tightly to shape tail.

House of White Birches, Berne, Indiana 46711 DRGnetwork.com

Beak

With smaller needles and G, cast on 6 sts.

Rows 1–3: Knit.

Row 4: [K2tog] across—3 sts.

Cut yarn, leaving long end. Draw end through all 3 sts and pull tight. Sew seam and sew in place.

Wing
Make 2

With smaller needles and E, cast on 15 sts.

Rows 1–4: Beg with knit row, work in St st.

Row 5: K2tog, knit to last 2 sts, k2tog—13 sts.

Row 6: Purl.

Rows 7–16: Rep [Rows 5 and 6] 5 times—3 sts.

Row 17: K3tog. Finish off, leaving long end for sewing.

Sew side seam. Stuff very loosely with fiberfill. Sew bottom opening closed. Sew wings in place.

Lion

With smaller needles and A, cast on 10 sts.

Rows 1–4: Knit.

Row 5: Knit, inc in each st across—20 sts.

Row 6: Purl.

Rows 7–22: Beg with knit row, work in St st.

Row 23: [K2, k2tog] 5 times—15 sts.

Row 24: Purl.

Row 25: [K1, k2tog] 5 times—10 sts.

Row 26: Purl.

Row 27: [K2tog] 5 times—5 sts.

Row 28: Purl.

Bind off.

Ear
Make 2

With A, cast on 4 sts.

Row 1: Knit.

Row 2: Purl.

Row 3: Knit.

Row 4: Purl.

Cut, leaving long end, draw through all sts on needle and pull tog tightly. Sew ears in place.

Finishing

With dark brown, embroider satin st eyes and nose, and straight st mouth.

Once Lion is sewn to afghan, with G embroider turkey st loops around face.

Elephant

With smaller needles and D, cast on 22 sts.

Row 1 (RS): Knit.

Row 2: Purl.

Row 3: K18, [k2tog] twice—20 sts.

Row 4: [P2tog] twice, p16—18 sts.

Row 5: K14, [k2tog] twice—16 sts.

Row 6: [P2tog] twice, p12—14 sts.

Row 7: Knit to last st, inc—15 sts.

Row 8: Purl.

Row 9: Cast on 2 sts, knit across—17 sts.

Row 10: Purl.

Rows 11–16: Beg with knit row, work in St st. *Note: Mark these rows for trunk placement.*

Row 17: Bind off 3 sts, knit to last 2 sts, k2tog—13 sts.

Row 18: Purl.

Row 19: K2tog, knit to last 2 sts, k2tog—11 sts.

Row 20: Purl.

Rows 21–26: Rep [Rows 19 and 20] 3 times—5 sts.

Bind off.

With dark brown, embroider satin st eye.

Once elephant is sewn to afghan, with D make 5 or 6 turkey st loops at top of head.

Tusk

With smaller needles and H, cast on 6 sts.

Row 1: Knit.

Row 2: P2tog, p2, p2tog—4 sts.

Row 3: Knit.

Row 4: [P2tog] twice—2 sts.

Row 5: K2tog—1 st.

Fold in half and sew seam, sew in place.

Ear

With smaller needles and D, cast on 10 sts.

Row 1: Knit.

Row 2: Purl.

Row 3: Knit, inc in each st across—20 sts.

Rows 4–8: Beg with purl row, work in St st.

Row 9: K2tog, k6, [k2tog] twice, k6, k2tog—16 sts.

Row 10: Purl.

Row 11: K2tog, k4, [k2tog] twice, k4, k2tog—12 sts.

Row 12: Purl.

Row 13: [K2tog] across.

Cut yarn, leaving long end for sewing, draw through all sts and pull tightly. Sew seam, and then sew ear in place.

Mouth

With smaller needles and D, cast on 8 sts.

Row 1: Knit.

Row 2: Purl.

Row 3: [K2tog] across—4 sts.

Gather sts tog and sew seam. Sew in place.

Trunk

Hold elephant with RS facing, with double-pointed needles and D pick up and knit 6 sts along Rows 11–16. Purl 1 row.

*K6, slide sts to opposite end of needle, pull yarn across back of work; rep from * until I-cord measures 2½ inches. Bind off.

Turtle

Shell

Make 1 each of A, D, E, F and H

With smaller needles, cast on 12 sts.

Rows 1 (RS)–3: Knit.

Row 4: Purl.

Row 5: K1, sl 1p, k1, psso, knit to last 3 sts, k2tog, k1—10 sts.

Row 6: Purl.

Rows 7–10: Rep [Rows 5 and 6] twice—6 sts.

Row 11: K1, sl 1p, k1, psso, k2tog, k1—4 sts.

Row 12: Purl.

Cut yarn, leaving a long end, draw end through all sts, pulling tightly.

Sew 5 triangles tog to form a circle.

Head

With smaller needles and C, cast on 7 sts.

Row 1: Knit.

Row 2: Purl.

Row 3: Knit, inc in each st across—14 sts.

Rows 4–6: Beg with purl row, work in St st.

Row 7: [K1, k2tog] twice, k2, [k2tog, k1] twice—10 sts.

Rows 8–12: Beg with purl row, work in St st.

Bind off, leaving long end for sewing.

Sew seam, stuffing loosely with fiberfill. Sew in place just under shell.

Leg
Make 4

With smaller needles and C, cast on 9 sts.

Rows 1–8: Beg with knit row, work in St st.

Cut, leaving a long end, draw through all sts. Sew seam and sew in place as for head.

Tail

With smaller needles and C, cast on 6 sts.

Rows 1–4: Beg with knit row, work in St st.

House of White Birches, Berne, Indiana 46711   DRGnetwork.com

Row 5: K2, k2tog, k2—5 sts.

Row 6: Purl.

Row 7: K1, k2tog, k2—3 sts.

Finish off leaving a long end, draw through rem sts. Do not stuff. Sew seam and sew in place.

Finishing
Embroider dark brown satin st eyes and straight st mouth.

Monkey

Front
Beg at top of head with smaller needles and H, cast on 8 sts.

Row 1 (RS): Knit.

Row 2: Purl.

Row 3: K1, inc, knit to last 2 sts, inc, k1—10 sts.

Row 4: Purl.

Rows 5–8: Rep [Rows 3 and 4] twice—14 sts.

Rows 9–16: Beg with knit row work in St st.

Row 17: [K2tog] across—7 sts.

Row 18: Purl.

Row 19: Knit, inc in each st across—14 sts.

Row 20: Purl.

Bind off.

Mouth Piece
With I, cast on 5 sts.

Row 1: Knit, inc in each st across—10 sts.

Row 2: Purl.

Rows 3–5: Knit.

Row 6: Purl.

Row 7: [K2tog] across—5 sts.

Row 8: Purl.

Bind off, leaving a long end for sewing.

Sew to front, stuffing lightly with fiberfill.

With dark brown, embroider a horizontal straight st under mouth line. Center a vertical straight st to hold mouth in place. Embroider satin st eyes and straight st nose.

Arm
Make 2

With H, cast on 8 sts.

Rows 1–20: Beg with knit row, work in St st.

Cut yarn, leaving a long end, draw through all sts and pull tightly. Sew seam, stuffing arm loosely with fiberfill. Sew arms in place.

Ear
Make 2

With I, cast on 3 sts.

Row 1: Knit, inc in each st across—6 sts.

Row 2: Purl.

Row 3: [K2tog] across—3 sts.

Cut yarn, leaving long end, draw through rem sts to pull tog. Sew ears in place.

Ark

Bottom of Ark
With smaller needles and C, cast on 50.

Row 1: Knit.

Row 2: K1, inc, knit to last 2 sts, inc, k1—52 sts.

Rows 3–10: Rep [Rows 1 and 2] 4 times—60 sts.

Row 11: Knit.

Row 12: K3, purl to last 3 sts, k3.

Rows 13 and 14: Rep Rows 11 and 12.

Rows 15 and 16: Knit.

Rows 17–40: Rep [Rows 11–16] 4 times.

Rows 41–50: [K2, p2] across.

Bind off in ribbing.

Ark Cabin
With smaller needles and I, cast on 25 sts.

Row 1 (RS): Knit.

Row 2: Purl.

Rows 3–6: Rep [Rows 1 and 2] twice.

continued on page 29

Gerry the Giraffe

Design by Michele Wilcox

Skill Level

◼◼◻◻ EASY

Finished Size

Approx 4 inches wide x 12 inches tall

Materials

- Plymouth Encore Worsted 75% acrylic/25% wool worsted weight yarn (200 yds/100g per ball): 1 ball fuchsia #137; small amount sage green #451 and denim blue #515
- Dark brown size 10 crochet thread or pearl cotton
- Size 5 (3.75mm) straight needles or size needed to obtain gauge
- Tapestry needle
- Fiberfill
- Safety pins (optional)

4 MEDIUM

Gauge

5 sts = 1 inch/2.5cm in St st.
To save time, take time to check gauge.

Special Abbreviation

Increase (inc): Inc 1 st by knitting in front and back of next st.

Front

Beg at top of head with fuchsia, cast on 8 sts.

Row 1 (RS): Knit.

Row 2: Purl.

Row 3: Inc, knit to last st, inc—10 sts.

Row 4: Purl.

Rows 5–8: Rep [Rows 3 and 4] twice—14 sts.

Row 9: Knit.

Row 10: Purl.

Row 11: Cast on 3 sts, knit across—17 sts.

Row 12: Purl.

Row 13: Inc, knit across—18 sts.

Row 14: Purl.

Row 15: Knit.

Row 16: Purl.

Row 17: K2tog, knit across—17 sts.

Row 18: Purl.

Row 19: Bind off 3 sts, knit across—14 sts.

Row 20: Purl to last 2 sts, p2tog—13 sts.

Row 21: K2tog, knit across—12 sts.

Rows 22–28: Beg with purl row, work in St st.

Row 29: K1, inc, k10—13 sts.

Row 30: Purl.

Row 31: K11, inc, k1—14 sts.

Row 32: Purl.

Row 33: K1, inc, k12—15 sts.

Row 34: Purl.

Row 35: K13, inc, k1—16 sts.

Row 36: Purl.

Row 37: K1, inc, k14—17 sts.

Row 38: Purl.

Row 39: K15, inc, k1—18 sts.

Rows 40–44: Beg with purl row, work in St st.

Row 45: Knit to last 2 sts, inc, k1—19 sts.

Row 46: Purl.

Rows 47–50: Rep [Rows 45 and 46] twice—21 sts.

Row 51: Rep Row 45—22 sts.

Row 52: Cast on 3 sts, purl across—25 sts.

Rows 53–74: Beg with knit row, work in St st. Bind off.

Back
With fuchsia, cast on 8 sts.

Rows 1–10: Work same as Rows 1–10 of Front.

Row 11: Knit.

Row 12: Cast on 3 sts, purl across—17 sts.

Row 13: K16, inc—18 sts.

Row 14: Purl.

Row 15: Knit.

Row 16: Purl.

Row 17: Knit to last 2 sts, k2tog—17 sts.

Row 18: Purl.

Row 19: Knit.

Row 20: Bind off 3 sts, p2tog, purl across—13 sts.

Row 21: Knit to last 2 sts, k2tog—12 sts.

Rows 22–44: Rep Rows 22–44 of Front.

Row 45: K1, inc, knit across—19 sts.

Row 46: Purl.

Rows 47–52: Rep [Rows 45 and 46] 3 times—22 sts.

Row 53: Cast on 3 sts, knit across—25 sts.

Rows 54–74: Beg with purl row, work in St st.

Bind off.

Spots
Make 6

With green, cast on 3 sts.

Row 1: Knit, inc in each st across—6 sts.

Row 2: Knit.

Row 3: [K2tog] 3 times—3 sts.

Bind off.

Finishing
Sew 3 spots to each side of giraffe.

Using safety pins, pin sides of giraffe tog (this will make it much easier to sew), sew sides tog, but do not sew across bottom. Stuff loosely with fiberfill. Sew across bottom.

To shape legs: With side of giraffe facing you, sew through all thicknesses from center bottom up about 2½ inches. Rep with front of giraffe facing you, sewing into the front and back seams to create 4 legs.

Ear
Make 2

With fuchsia, cast on 6 sts.

Row 1: Knit.

Row 2: Purl.

Row 3: Knit, inc in each st across—12 sts.

Rows 4–8: Beg with a purl row, work in St st.

Row 9: [K2tog] across—6 sts.

Row 10: Purl.

Row 11: [K2tog] across—3 sts.

Row 12: Purl.

Cut yarn, leaving a long end, thread end through sts and pull tightly. Sew back seam. Do not stuff. Fold Row 1 in half and sew ears in place.

Horn
Make 2

With green, cast on 5 sts.

Row 1: Knit.

Row 2: Purl.

Cut yarn, leaving a long end, draw through sts on needle and pull tightly. Sew seam and sew in place.

Mane
With blue, embroider turkey st loops (see page 31) along neck edge.

Face
With dark brown, embroider satin st eyes and straight st smile (see page 31).

Tail
With fuchsia, cast on 9 sts. Bind off. Sew in place. ∎

House of White Birches, Berne, Indiana 46711   DRGnetwork.com

Freddie the Fish

Design by Michele Wilcox

Skill Level

■■□□ EASY

Finished Size

Approx 6½ inches long x 3½ inches high

Materials

- Plymouth Encore Worsted 75% acrylic/25% wool worsted weight yarn (200 yds/100g per ball): 1 ball orange #1316
- Dark brown size 10 crochet thread or pearl cotton
- Size 5 (3.75mm) knitting needles or size needed to obtain gauge
- Tapestry needle
- Fiberfill

Gauge

5 sts = 1 inch/2.5cm in St st.
To save time, take time to check gauge.

Special Abbreviation

Increase (inc): Inc by knitting in front and back of next st.

Side

Make 2

With orange, cast on 3 sts.

Row 1 (RS): Knit.

Row 2: Purl.

Row 3: Knit, inc in each st across—6 sts.

Row 4: Purl.

Row 5: Inc, knit to last st, inc—8 sts.

Row 6: Purl.

Row 7: Rep Row 5—10 sts.

Rows 8 and 9: Knit.

Row 10: Purl.

Row 11: Rep Row 5—12 sts.

Rows 12 and 13: Knit.

Row 14: Purl.

Row 15: Rep Row 5—14 sts.

Rows 16 and 17: Knit.

Row 18: Purl.

Row 19: Rep Row 5—16 sts.

Rows 20 and 21: Knit.

Row 22: Purl.

Rows 23–25: Knit.

Row 26: Purl.

Rows 27–29: Knit.

Row 30: Purl.

Row 31: *K2, k2tog; rep from * across—12 sts.

Row 32: Knit.

Row 33: *K1, k2tog; rep from * across—8 sts.

Row 34: Purl.

Row 35: [K2tog] across—4 sts.

Row 36: Knit.

Rows 37–40: Beg with knit row, work in St st.

Row 41: Knit, inc in each st across—8 sts.

Row 42: Purl.

Row 43: Rep Row 41—16 sts.

Row 44: Purl.

Row 45: Inc, knit to last st, inc—18 sts.

Rows 46–50: Beg with purl row, work in St st.

Bind off.

Finishing

Sew sides tog, stuffing loosely with fiberfill before closing.

With dark brown, embroider satin st eye on each side and straight st smile (see page 31).

Run a piece of yarn 5 rows down from center of tail around center of tail and through again, pull tightly to shape tail. Tie tightly and work ends inside of tail.

Top Fin

With orange, cast on 10 sts.

Row 1: [K2, p2] twice, k2.

Row 2: [P2, k2] twice, p2.

Rows 3–8: Rep [Rows 1 and 2] 3 times.

Bind off in ribbing. Fold in half and sew in place.

Side Fin
Make 2

With orange, cast on 3 sts.

Row 1: Knit, inc in each st across—6 sts.

Row 2: Purl.

Row 3: Knit.

Row 4: Purl.

Row 5: [K2tog] across—3 sts.

Cut yarn, leaving long end, draw through rem sts and pull tightly. Sew fin on each side. ∎

Bobby the Bluebird

Design by Michele Wilcox

Skill Level

 EASY

Finished Size

Approx 8 inches long x 7 inches across from wing to wing

Materials

- Plymouth Encore Worsted 75% acrylic/25% wool worsted weight yarn (200 yds/100g per ball): 1 ball denim blue #515; small amount orange #1316
- Dark brown size 10 crochet thread or pearl cotton
- Size 5 (3.75mm) straight needles or size needed to obtain gauge
- Tapestry needle
- Fiberfill

Gauge

5 sts = 1 inch in St st.
To save time, take time to check gauge.

Special Abbreviation

Increase (inc): Inc 1 st by knitting in front and back of next st.

Top/Bottom

Beg at head end, with blue, cast on 4 sts.

Row 1 (RS): Inc, knit to last st, inc—6 sts.

Row 2: Purl.

Rows 3–6: Rep [Rows 1 and 2] twice—10 sts.

Rows 7–10: Beg with knit row, work in St st.

Row 11: [K2tog] across—5 sts.

Row 12: Purl.

Row 13: Knit, inc in each st across—10 sts.

Row 14: Purl.

Row 15: Rep Row 1—12 sts.

Row 16: Purl.

Row 17: Rep Row 1—14 sts.

Rows 18–32: Beg with purl row, work in St st.

Row 33: K2tog, knit to last 2 sts, k2tog—12 sts.

Row 34: Purl.

Row 35: Rep Row 33—10 sts.

Row 36: Purl.

Row 37: Rep Row 33—8 sts.

Rows 38–44: Beg with purl row, work in St st.

Row 45: Rep Row 1—10 sts.

Row 46: Purl.

Row 47: Rep Row 1—12 sts.

Row 48: Purl.

Row 49: Rep Row 1—14 sts.

Row 50: Purl.

Bind off.

Finishing

Pin the top and bottom pieces tog and sew, leaving tail area open. Stuff loosely with fiberfill and sew tail closed.

With dark brown, embroider satin st eyes (see page 31).

Run a piece of blue yarn 3 rows down from center of tail around center of tail and through again, pull tightly to shape tail. Tie tightly and work ends inside of tail.

Beak

With orange, cast on 6 sts.

Rows 1–3: Knit.

Row 4: [K2tog] across—3 sts.

Cut yarn, leaving long end, draw through all 3 sts on needle and pull tight. Sew seam and sew in place.

Wing
Make 2

With blue, cast on 15 sts.

Rows 1 (RS)–4: Beg with knit row, work in St st.

Row 5: K2tog, knit to last 2 sts, k2tog—13 sts.

Row 6: Purl.

Rows 7–16: Rep [Rows 5 and 6] 5 times—3 sts.

Row 17: K3tog. Finish off, leaving a long end for sewing.

Sew side seam. Stuff very loosely with fiberfill. Sew bottom opening closed. Sew wings in place. ■

Flying High Pillow

Designs by Michele Wilcox

Skill Level

 EASY

Finished Size

12 inches square

Materials

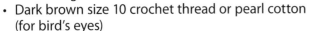

- Plymouth Encore Worsted 75% acrylic/25% wool worsted weight yarn (200 yds/100g per ball): 2 balls yellow #215; small amount denim blue #515 and orange #1316
- Dark brown size 10 crochet thread or pearl cotton (for bird's eyes)
- Size 5 (3.75mm) knitting needles or size needed to obtain gauge
- Size 9 (5.25mm) knitting needles or size needed to obtain gauge
- Tapestry needle
- Small amount of fiberfill (for bird)
- Pillow form

Gauge

15 sts = 4 inches/10cm with larger needles in pat st.
20 sts = 4 inches/10cm with smaller needles in St st.
To save time, take time to check gauge.

Special Abbreviation

Increase (inc): Inc by knitting in front and back of next st.

Pillow

Front/Back

Make 2

With larger needles and yellow, cast on 49 sts.

Row 1 (RS): Knit.

Row 2: K1, *p7, k1; rep from * across.

Row 3: K4, *p1, k7; rep from * to last 5 sts, p1, k4.

Row 4: K1, *p2, k1, p1, k1, p2, k1; rep from * across.

Row 5: K2, *[p1, k1] twice, p1, k3; rep from * to last 7 sts, [p1, k1] twice, p1, k2.

Row 6: Rep Row 4.

Row 7: Rep Row 3.

Row 8: Rep Row 2.

Rows 9–72: Rep [Rows 1–8] 8 times. Bind off.

Bird

Body

Beg at head, with smaller needles and blue cast on 4 sts.

Row 1: Inc, knit to last st, inc—6 sts.

Row 2: Purl.

Rows 3–6: Rep [Rows 1 and 2] twice—10 sts.

Rows 7–10: Beg with knit row, work in St st.

Row 11: [K2tog] across—5 sts.

Row 12: Purl.

Row 13: Knit, inc in each st across—10 sts.

Row 14: Purl.

Row 15: Rep Row 1—12 sts.

Row 16: Purl.

Row 17: Rep Row 1—14 sts.

Rows 18–32: Beg with purl row, work in St st.

Row 33: K2tog, knit to last 2 sts, k2tog—12 sts.

Row 34: Purl.

Row 35: Rep Row 33—10 sts.

Row 36: Purl.

Row 37: Rep Row 33—8 sts.

Rows 38–44: Beg with purl row, work in St st.

Row 45: Rep Row 1—10 sts.

Row 46: Purl.

Row 47: Rep Row 1—12 sts.

Row 48: Purl.

Row 49: Rep Row 1—14 sts.

Row 50: Purl.

Bind off.

With dark brown, embroider satin st (see page 31 eyes).

Run a piece of blue yarn 3 rows down from center of tail around center of tail and through again, pull tightly to shape tail.

Beak
With smaller needles and orange, cast on 6 sts.

Rows 1–3: Knit.

Row 4: [K2tog] across—3 sts.

Cut yarn, leaving long end, draw through all 3 sts on needle and pull tight. Sew seam and sew in place.

Wing
Make 2

With smaller needles and blue, cast on 15 sts.

Rows 1–4: Beg with knit row, work in St st.

Row 5: K2tog, knit to last 2 sts, k2tog—13 sts.

Row 6: Purl.

Rows 7–16: Rep [Rows 5 and 6] 5 times—3 sts.

Row 17: K3tog. Finish off, leaving a long end for sewing.

Sew side seam. Stuff very loosely with fiberfill. Sew bottom opening closed. Sew wings in place.

Finishing
Sew bird onto center of pillow front placing a small amount of fiberfill under the head and body.

Sew pillow front to back tog along 3 sides. Insert pillow form and sew rem side. ■

House of White Birches, Berne, Indiana 46711 DRGnetwork.com

Leo the Lion

Design by Michele Wilcox

Gauge
5 sts = 1 inch/2.5cm in St st.
To save time, take time to check gauge.

Special Abbreviation
Increase (inc): Inc 1 st by knitting in front and back of next st.

Side
Make 2

Beg at bottom of legs with yellow, cast on 20 sts.

Rows 1 (RS)–6: Knit.

Row 7: K1, k2tog, knit to last 3 sts, k2tog, k1—18 sts.

Rows 8–22: Beg with purl row, work in St st.

Row 23: [K2tog] across—9 sts.

Row 24: Knit.

Row 25: Knit, inc in each st across—18 sts.

Row 26: Purl.

Row 27: K1, inc, knit to last 2 sts, inc, k1—20 sts.

Row 28: Purl.

Rows 29–44: Beg with knit row, work in St st.

Row 45: [K2, k2tog] 5 times—15 sts.

Row 46: Purl.

Row 47: [K1, k2tog] 5 times—10 sts.

Row 48: Purl.

Row 49: [K2tog] 5 times—5 sts.

Row 50: Purl.

Bind off.

Ear
Make 2

With yellow, cast on 4 sts.

Row 1: Knit.

Row 2: Purl.

Skill Level
■■□□ EASY

Finished Size
Approx 7½ inches (including mane) tall x 4 inches wide

Materials
- Plymouth Encore Worsted 75% acrylic/25% wool worsted weight yarn (200 yds/100g per ball): 1 ball yellow #215; small amount orange #1316
- Dark brown size 10 crochet thread or pearl cotton
- Size 5 (3.75mm) knitting needles or size needed to obtain gauge
- Tapestry needle
- Fiberfill

4 MEDIUM

Row 3: Knit.

Row 4: Purl.

Cut, leaving long end, draw through all sts on needle and pull tog tightly. Sew ears in place.

For tassel: Cut 8 (5-inch) lengths of orange. Tie 1 length around center of 6 lengths. Fold in half and tie another length around all strands ½ inch from fold. Tie tassel to end of tail.

Sew tail in place.

With orange embroider turkey st loops (see page 31) around face. ■

Tail
With yellow, cast on 10 sts.

Row 1: Knit.

Bind off.

Finishing
With dark brown embroider satin st eyes and nose, and straight st mouth (see page 31).

Sew back to front tog, stuffing loosely with fiberfill before closing. Form legs by working back st through all thicknesses from bottom center of lion up about 1½ inch.

Terry the Turtle

Design by Michele Wilcox

Skill Level

◼◼◻◻ **EASY**

Finished Size

Approx 7 inches long from head to tail

Materials

- Plymouth Encore Worsted 75% acrylic/25% wool worsted weight yarn (200 yds/100g per ball): small amount each teal #9401, sage green #451, pink heather #241, dusty purple #452, yellow #215, fuchsia #137 and denim blue #515
- Dark brown size 10 crochet thread or pearl cotton
- Size 5 (3.75mm) knitting needles or size needed to obtain gauge
- Tapestry needle
- Fiberfill

4 MEDIUM

Gauge

5 sts = 1 inch/2.5cm in St st.
To save time, take time to check gauge.

Special Abbreviation

Increase (inc): Inc by knitting in front and back of next st.

Shell

Make 1 triangle section each of pink, purple, yellow, fuchsia and blue.

Cast on 12 sts.

Rows 1 (RS)–3: Knit.

Row 4: Purl.

Row 5: K1, sl 1p, k1, psso, knit to last 3 sts, k2tog, k1—10 sts.

Row 6: Purl.

Rows 7–10: Rep [Rows 5 and 6] twice—6 sts.

Row 11: K1, sl 1p, k1, psso, k2tog, k1—4 sts.

Row 12: Purl.

Cut yarn, leaving a long end, draw through all sts on needle and pull tightly.

Sew 5 triangles tog to form a circle.

Turtle bottom

With teal, cast on 12 sts.

Row 1: Knit.

Row 2: Purl.

Row 3: K1, inc, knit to last 2 sts, inc, k1—14 sts.

Row 4: Purl.

Rows 5–10: Rep [Rows 3 and 4] 3 times—20 sts.

Rows 11–16: Beg with knit row, work in St st.

Row 17: K1, sl 1p, k1, psso, knit to last 3 sts, k2tog, k1—18 sts.

Row 18: Purl.

Rows 19–24: Rep [Rows 17 and 18] 3 times—12 sts.

Bind off.

Head

With green, cast on 7 sts.

Row 1: Knit.

Row 2: Purl.

Row 3: Knit, inc in each st acros—14 sts.

Rows 4–6: Beg with purl row, work in St st.

Row 7: [K1, k2tog] twice, k2, [k2tog, k1] twice—10 sts.

Rows 8–12: Beg with purl row, work in St st.

Bind off, leaving a long end for sewing.

Sew seam, stuffing loosely with fiberfill. Sew in place just under shell.

Leg

Make 4

With green, cast on 9 sts.

Rows 1–8: Beg with knit row, work in St st.

Cut, leaving a long end, draw through all sts pulling tog. Sew seam, stuffing loosely with fiberfill and sew in place as for head.

Tail

With green, cast on 6 sts.

Rows 1–4: Beg with knit row, work in St st.

Row 5: K2, k2tog, k2—5 sts.

Row 6: Purl.

Row 7: K1, k2tog, k2—3 sts.

Finish off leaving a long end, draw through rem sts pulling tog. Do not stuff. Sew seam and sew in place.

Finishing

Embroider dark brown satin st eyes and straight st mouth (see page 31). ■

House of White Birches, Berne, Indiana 46711   DRGnetwork.com

Madeleine the Monkey

Design by Michele Wilcox

Gauge

5 sts = 1 inch/2.5cm in St st.
To save time, take time to check gauge.

Special Abbreviation

Increase (inc): Inc by knitting in front and back of next st.

Front/Back

Beg at top of head with pink heather, cast on 8 sts.

Row 1 (RS): Knit.

Row 2: Purl.

Row 3: K1, inc, knit to last 2 sts, inc, k1—10 sts.

Row 4: Purl.

Rows 5–8: Rep [Rows 3 and 4] twice—14 sts.

Rows 9–16: Beg with knit row, work in St st.

Row 17: [K2tog] across—7 sts.

Row 18: Purl.

Row 19: Knit, inc in each st across—14 sts.

Row 20: Purl.

Row 21: Rep Row 3—16 sts.

Row 22: Purl.

Rows 23–36: Beg with knit row, work in St st.

Row 37: K1, [k2 tog] 3 times, k2, [k2tog] 3 times, k1—10 sts.

Row 38: Purl.

Bind off.

Mouth Piece

With tan, cast on 5 sts.

Row 1: Knit inc in each st across—10 sts.

Row 2: Purl.

Skill Level

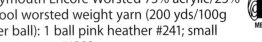 EASY

Finished Size

Approx 8 inches tall, excluding tail

Materials

- Plymouth Encore Worsted 75% acrylic/25% wool worsted weight yarn (200 yds/100g per ball): 1 ball pink heather #241; small amount tan #1203
- Dark brown size 10 crochet thread or pearl cotton
- Size 5 (3.75mm) knitting needles or size needed to obtain gauge
- Tapestry needle
- Fiberfill

4 MEDIUM

Rows 3–5: Knit.

Row 6: Purl.

Row 7: [K2tog] across—5 sts.

Row 8: Purl.

Bind off.

Sew to front, stuffing lightly with fiberfill.

With dark brown, embroider a horizontal straight st under mouth line. Center a vertical straight st to hold mouth in place. Embroider satin st eyes and straight st nose (see page 31).

Leg
Make 2

With pink heather, cast on 10 sts.

Rows 1–16: Beg with knit row, work in St st.

Cut yarn, leaving a long end, draw end through all sts and pull tightly. Sew seam, stuffing leg loosely with fiberfill. Sew legs in place.

Arm
Make 2

With pink heather, cast on 8 sts.

Rows 1–20: Beg with knit row, work in St st.

Cut yarn, leaving a long end, draw end through all sts and pull tightly. Sew seam, stuffing arm loosely with fiberfill. Sew arms in place.

Ear
Make 2

With tan, cast on 3 sts.

Row 1: Knit, inc in each st across—6 sts.

Row 2: Purl.

Row 3: [K2tog] across—3 sts.

Cut yarn, leaving long end, draw end through rem sts to pull tog. Sew ears in place.

Tail
With pink heather, cast on 6 sts.

Rows 1–26: Beg with knit row, work in St st.

Cut yarn, leaving a long end, draw end through all sts and pull tightly. Sew seam and sew in place. ■

Ellie the Elephant

Design by Michele Wilcox

Skill Level

 ■■□□ EASY

Finished Size

Approx 9 inches tall

Materials

- Plymouth Encore Worsted 75% acrylic/25% wool worsted weight yarn (200 yds/100g per ball): 1 ball dusty purple #452; small amount pink heather #241
- Dark brown size 10 crochet thread or pearl cotton
- Size 5 (3.75mm) straight needles or size needed to obtain gauge
- Tapestry needle
- Fiberfill
- Safety pins (optional)

Gauge

5 sts = 1 inch/2.5cm in St st.
To save time, take time to check gauge.

Special Abbreviation
Increase (inc): Inc 1 st by knitting in front and back of next st.

First Side
Beg at bottom of feet, with purple, cast on 20 sts.

Row 1 (RS): *K2, p2; rep from * across.

Rows 2–4: Rep Row 1.

Row 5: [K3, inc] 5 times—25 sts.

Rows 6–28: Beg with a purl row, work in St st.

Row 29: Inc, k20, [k2tog] twice—24 sts.

Row 30: Purl.

Row 31: Inc, k19, [k2tog] twice—23 sts.

Row 32: Purl.

Row 33: Inc, k18, [k2tog] twice—22 sts.

Row 34: Purl.

Row 35: K18, [k2tog] twice—20 sts.

Row 36: [P2tog] twice, p16—18 sts.

Row 37: K14, [k2tog] twice—16 sts.

Row 38: [P2tog] twice, p12—14 sts.

Row 39: Knit to last st, inc—15 sts.

Row 40: Purl.

Row 41: Cast on 7 sts, knit across—22 sts.

Row 42: Purl.

Rows 43–48: Beg with knit row, work in St st.

Row 49: Bind off 8 sts, knit to last 2 sts, k2tog—13 sts.

Row 50: Purl.

Row 51: K2tog, knit to last 2 sts, k2tog—11 sts.

Row 52: Purl.

Rows 53–58: Rep [Rows 51 and 52] 3 times—5 sts.
Bind off.

Second Side
Rows 1–28: Work same as Rows 1–28 of First Side.

Row 29: [K2tog] twice, k20, inc—24 sts.

Row 30: Purl across.

Row 31: [K2tog] twice, k19, inc—23 sts.

Row 32: Purl across.

Row 33: [K2tog] twice, k18, inc—22 sts.

Row 34: Purl across.

Row 35: [K2tog] twice, k18—20 sts.

Row 36: P16, [p2tog] twice—18 sts.

Row 37: [K2tog] twice, k14—16 sts.

Row 38: P12, [p2tog] twice—14 sts.

Row 39: Inc, knit across—15 sts.

Row 40: Cast on 7 sts, purl across—22 sts.

Rows 41–47: Beg with knit row, work in St st.

Row 48: Bind off 8 sts, purl across—13 sts.

Row 49: Knit.

Rows 50–58: Work same as Rows 50–58 of First Side.

Finishing
Using safety pins, pin sides of elephant tog (this will make it much easier to sew), sew sides tog, but do not sew across bottom. Stuff loosely with fiberfill and sew across bottom.

To shape legs: With side of elephant facing you, sew through all thicknesses from center bottom up about 2½ inches. Rep with front of elephant facing you, sewing into the front and back seams to create 4 legs.

With dark brown embroider satin st eyes (see page 31).

With purple make 5 or 6 turkey st loops at top of head (see page 31).

Tusk
Make 2

With pink, cast on 6 sts.

Row 1: Knit.

Row 2: P2tog, p2, p2tog—4 sts.

Row 3: Knit.

Row 4: [P2tog] twice—2 sts.

Row 5: K2tog—1 st.

Fold in half and sew seam, sew in place.

Tail

With purple cast on 9 sts.

Bind off.

For tassel: Cut 8 (5-inch) lengths of purple. Tie 1 length around center of 6 lengths. Fold yarn in half and tie another length around all strands ½ inch from fold. Tie tassel to end of tail. Sew in place.

Ear
Make 2

With purple, cast on 10 sts.

Row 1: Knit.

Row 2: Purl.

Row 3: Knit, inc in each st across—20 sts.

Rows 4–8: Beg with purl row, work in St st.

Row 9: K2tog, k6, [k2tog] twice, k6, k2tog—16 sts.

Row 10: Purl.

Row 11: K2tog, k4, [k2tog] twice, k4, k2tog—12 sts.

Row 12: Purl.

Row 13: [K2tog] across.

Cut yarn, leaving length for sewing, draw through all sts on needle and pull tightly. Sew seam and sew ear in place.

Mouth

With purple, cast on 8 sts.

Row 1: Knit.

Row 2: Purl.

Row 3: [K2tog] across—4 sts.

Finish off, leaving a long end, draw through all sts on needle and gather tog. Sew seam and sew in place. ■

Noah's Ark Afghan

Continued from page 10

Rows 7–9: Knit.

Row 10: Purl.

Row 11: Knit.

Rows 12 and 13: Rep Rows 10 and 11.

Rows 14 and 15: Knit.

Rows 16–27: Rep [Rows 10–15] twice.

Bind off.

Ark Roof
With smaller needles and C, cast on 30 sts.

Rows 1 (RS)–3: Knit.

Row 4: K4, purl to last 4 sts, k4.

Row 5: K1, k2tog, knit to last 3 sts, k2tog, k1—28 sts.

Rows 6–13: Rep [Rows 4 and 5] 4 times—20 sts.

Rows 14–16: Knit.

Bind off.

Finishing
Referring to photo for placement, position ark and all animals on afghan. Sew in place, with background pieces first and others added on top. ■

General Information

Inches into Millimetres & Centimetres

All measurements are rounded off slightly.

inches	mm	cm	inches	cm	inches	cm	inches	cm	inches	cm
⅛	3	0.3	3	7.5	13	33.0	26	66.0	39	99.0
¼	6	0.6	3½	9.0	14	35.5	27	68.5	40	101.5
⅜	10	1.0	4	10.0	15	38.0	28	71.0	41	104.0
½	13	1.3	4½	11.5	16	40.5	29	73.5	42	106.5
⅝	15	1.5	5	12.5	17	43.0	30	76.0	43	109.0
¾	20	2.0	5½	14	18	46.0	31	79.0	44	112.0
⅞	22	2.2	6	15.0	19	48.5	32	81.5	45	114.5
1	25	2.5	7	18.0	20	51.0	33	84.0	46	117.0
1¼	32	3.8	8	20.5	21	53.5	34	86.5	47	119.5
1½	38	3.8	9	23.0	22	56.0	35	89.0	48	122.0
1¾	45	4.5	10	25.5	23	58.5	36	91.5	49	124.5
2	50	5.0	11	28.0	24	61.0	37	94.0	50	127.0
2½	65	6.5	12	30.5	25	63.5	38	96.5		

House of White Birches, Berne, Indiana 46711   DRGnetwork.com

Abbreviations & Symbols

[ ] work instructions within brackets as many times as directed

( ) · · · · work instructions within parentheses in the place directed

** · repeat instructions following the asterisks as directed

* · repeat instructions following the single asterisk as directed

" · · · · · · · · · · · inch(es)

approx · · · · · ·approximately

beg · · · · · · ·begin/beginning

CC · · · · · · ·contrasting color

ch · · · · · · · · · chain stitch

cm · · · · · · · · · centimeter(s)

cn · · · · · · · · · cable needle

dec · decrease/decreases/decreasing

dpn(s) · · double-pointed needle(s)

g · · · · · · · · · · · · gram

inc · ·increase/increases/increasing

k · · · · · · · · · · · · · knit

k2tog · · · knit 2 stitches together

LH · · · · · · · · · · left hand

lp(s) · · · · · · · · · loop(s)

m · · · · · · · · · · meter(s)

M1 · · · · · · make one stitch

MC · · · · · · · main color

mm · · · · · · · ·millimeter(s)

oz · · · · · · · · · ounce(s)

p · · · · · · · · · · · ·purl

pat(s) · · · · · ·pattern(s)

p2tog · · purl 2 stitches together

psso · · · pass slipped stitch over

p2sso · ·pass 2 slipped stitches over

rem · · · · · · remain/remaining

rep · · · · · · · · · repeat(s)

rev St st ·reverse stockinette stitch

RH · · · · · · · · · right hand

rnd(s) · · · · · · · · ·rounds

RS · · · · · · · · · right side

skp slip, knit, pass stitch over—one stitch decreased

sk2p slip 1, knit 2 together, pass slip stitch over the knit 2 together—2 stitches have been decreased

sl · · · · · · · · · · · · slip

sl 1k · · · · · · · slip 1 knitwise

sl 1p · · · · · · · slip 1 purlwise

sl st · · · · · · · slip stitch(es)

ssk slip, slip, knit these 2 stitches together—a decrease

st(s) · · · · · · · · · stitch(es)

St st · · · · · · stockinette stitch/stocking stitch

tbl · · · · · through back loop(s)

tog · · · · · · · · · together

WS · · · · · · · · · wrong side

wyib · · · · · ·with yarn in back

wyif · · · · ·with yarn in front

yd(s) · · · · · · · · · yard(s)

yfwd · · · · · · yarn forward

yo · · · · · · · · ·yarn over

Standard Yarn Weight System

Categories of yarn, gauge ranges, and recommended needle sizes

Yarn Weight Symbol & Category Names	① SUPER FINE	② FINE	③ LIGHT	④ MEDIUM	⑤ BULKY	⑥ SUPER BULKY
Type of Yarns in Category	Sock, Fingering, Baby	Sport, Baby	DK, Light Worsted	Worsted, Afghan, Aran	Chunky, Craft, Rug	Bulky, Roving
Knit Gauge Range* in Stockinette Stitch to 4 inches	27–32 sts	23–26 sts	21–24 sts	16–20 sts	12–15 sts	6–11 sts
Recommended Needle in Metric Size Range	2.25–3.25mm	3.25–3.75mm	3.75–4.5mm	4.5–5.5mm	5.5–8mm	8mm and larger
Recommended Needle U.S. Size Range	1 to 3	3 to 5	5 to 7	7 to 9	9 to 11	11 and larger

* GUIDELINES ONLY: The above reflect the most commonly used gauges and needle sizes for specific yarn categories.

Embroidery Stitches

Turkey Stitch

Come up at A, leaving a length of yarn on WS.

Make a loop of desired length by going down at D.

Bring needle up at B and go down at C to lock loop in place.

Then bring needle up at E and down at B.

Continue for required number of loops.

Use a free finger, knitting needle or pencil for consistent-sized loops.

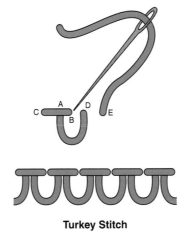

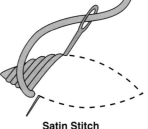

Satin Stitch

Straight Stitch

Turkey Stitch

Skill Levels

BEGINNER

Beginner projects for first-time knitters using basic stitches. Minimal shaping.

EASY

Easy projects using basic stitches, repetitive stitch patterns, simple color changes, and simple shaping and finishing.

INTERMEDIATE

Intermediate projects with a variety of stitches, mid-level shaping and finishing.

EXPERIENCED

Experienced projects using advanced techniques and stitches, detailed shaping and refined finishing.

Knitting Needle Conversion Chart

U.S.	1	2	3	4	5	6	7	8	9	10	10½	11	13	15	17	19	35	50
Continental-mm	2.25	2.75	3.25	3.5	3.75	4	4.5	5	5.5	6	6.5	8	9	10	12.75	15	19	25

E-mail: Customer_Service@whitebirches.com

HOUSE of WHITE BIRCHES
PUBLISHERS SINCE 1947

Animal Friends Two by Two is published by DRG, 306 East Parr Road, Berne, IN 46711, telephone (260) 589-4000. Printed in USA. Copyright © 2009 DRG. All rights reserved. This publication may not be reproduced in part or in whole without written permission from the publisher.

RETAIL STORES: If you would like to carry this pattern book or any other DRG publications, call the Wholesale Department at Annie's Attic to set up a direct account: (903) 636-4303. Also, request a complete listing of publications available from DRG.

Every effort has been made to ensure that the instructions in this pattern book are complete and accurate. We cannot, however, take responsibility for human error, typographical mistakes or variations in individual work.

STAFF

Editor: Jeanne Stauffer
Managing Editor: Dianne Schmidt
Technical Editor: Kathy Wesley
Copy Supervisor: Michelle Beck
Copy Editors: Mary O'Donnell, Amanda Ladig , Susanna Tobias
Graphic Arts Supervisor: Ronda Bechinski

Graphic Artists: Erin Augsburger, Joanne Gonzalez
Art Director: Brad Snow
Assistant Art Director: Nick Pierce
Photography Supervisor: Tammy Christian
Photography: Matthew Owen
Photo Stylist: Tammy Steiner

ISBN: 978-1-59217-258-0

1 2 3 4 5 6 7 8 9

Photo Index

11

14

20

16

24

22

18

26